the guide to owning an
Australian Shepherd

W9-BFE-505

by Sheila Webster Boneham, Ph.D.

ASCA and AKC Ch. Brookridge Dustin U, AKC and ASCA CD, owned by author Sheila Webster Boneham.

© T.F.H. Publications, Inc.

Distributed in the UNITED STATES to the Pet Trade by T.F.H. Publications, Inc., 1 TFH Plaza, Neptune City, NJ 07753; on the Internet at www.tfh.com; in CANADA by Rolf C. Hagen Inc., 3225 Sartelon St., Montreal, Quebec H4R 1E8; Pet Trade by H & L Pet Supplies Inc., 27 Kingston Crescent, Kitchener, Ontario N2B 2T6; in ENGLAND by T.F.H. Publications, PO Box 74, Havant PO9 5TT; in AUSTRALIA AND THE SOUTH PACIFIC by T.F.H. (Australia), Pty. Ltd., Box 149, Brookvale 2100 N.S.W., Australia; in NEW ZEALAND by Brooklands Aquarium Ltd., 5 McGiven Drive, New Plymouth, RD1 New Zealand; in SOUTH AFRICA by Rolf C. Hagen S.A. (PTY.) LTD., P.O. Box 201199, Durban North 4016, South Africa; in JAPAN by T.F.H. Publications. Published by T.F.H. Publications, Inc.

**MANUFACTURED IN THE
UNITED STATES OF AMERICA
BY T.F.H. PUBLICATIONS, INC.**

Contents

The Publisher wishes to acknowledge the following owners of dogs in this book: Sheila Boneham, C. Briard, Kim Cochran, Becky Coon, Debbie Corrado, Heather Dickinson, Krista Dlugolecki, Deborah Dodds, Pamela Downs, Peggy Faith, Jack Feir, Gail Gardiner, Dr. Hennessy, A. L. Hicks, Michelle Kennedy, Anja Koperberg, Linda LaFrance, T. Ledutue, Caterina Lejeune, Kerry Levin-Smith, Jenna Mackey, Roberta Morrison, Ann New, Sandra Noell, Caterina O'Sullivan, Suzanne Ritter, Lois Rondeau, Jack Ryen, Glenda Stephenson, Pat Stout, Jill Termini, Kim Waldron, William Welty, Sarandria Whitacre

Photographers: Sheila Boneham, Paulette Braun, Isabelle Francais, Hammond Photography, Robert Pearcy, George Shagawat, Judith Strom

Sheila Webster Boneham, Ph.D., is an award-winning member of the Dog Writers Association of America. She breeds Australian Shepherds under the kennel name Perennial. Her Aussies keep her busy training and competing in several canine sports and making visits as therapy dogs.

Photo by Sheila Webster Boneham

Origins of the Australian Shepherd

WHAT IS AN AUSTRALIAN SHEPHERD?

Over the past few years, America has seemed to notice one of its finest natives—the Australian Shepherd, affectionately known to his fans as the "Aussie." The handsome Aussie suddenly seems to be everywhere we look: in advertising, in televised canine sporting events, and out in public. At a glance, his medium size, his high intelligence, his willingness to obey, his athleticism, and his beauty make the Australian Shepherd an ideal canine companion. In the right environment, the Aussie is, as his many fans proclaim, "aussome." But before you decide to get an Aussie, please read on. The Australian Shepherd is not for everyone.

The ideal Australian Shepherd ranges in size from 18 to 23 inches in height and 35 to 70 pounds, although some individuals are slightly smaller or larger. Females generally are smaller (18 to 21 inches) than males (20 to 23 inches), and males and females should appear masculine and feminine, respectively. The Aussie carries a moderately long double coat on the body, with smooth hair on the head and face. Males are adorned with a heavier mane and

The Australian Shepherd developed in North America. It is believed the breed is descended from sheepherding dogs that accompanied Basque shepherds who came to the US in the late 1800s.

ruff. The outer coat should be straight or wavy, although curly coats show up on occasion. The downy undercoat is short and dense, and protects the skin from scratches and the elements. Aussies come in four colors—black, blue merle, red, and red merle—with or without white and copper trim.

Aussies are extremely athletic and agile and demonstrate tremendous stamina, strength, and courage. The Aussie is known for his delightful sense of fun and is commonly called "wriggle-butt" for the way he wags his entire body, right down to the natural or docked bobtail. Bred to be a working dog with strong herding and guarding instincts, the Australian Shepherd needs training, lots of exercise, and a job to do. The Aussie must have activities to engage his mind and body—if you don't provide them, he'll find some for himself, and you probably won't like his idea of fun!

HISTORY OF THE AUSTRALIAN SHEPHERD

The Australian Shepherd developed in North America. Although theories on the Aussie's origins vary to some degree, it is generally accepted that the breed is descended from the sheepherding dogs that accompanied Basque shepherds who came to the US in the late 1800s and early 1900s. Large flocks of sheep were imported during those years from Australia, New Zealand, Britain, Spain, and France. Along with their sheep- herding expertise, the Basques also brought their "little blue dogs." American ranchers and farmers, impressed by the working abilities of these bobtailed dogs, began using them as all-around ranch hands. Dogs were selected for breeding based on their abilities, and other herding breeds were crossed with the Basque-type dogs in order to get certain traits. The Aussie of today is recognizably related to a number of breeds around the world, including the German Coolie (collie) in Australia, the Welsh Bobtail, the Irish Collie, and certain European breeds.

Eventually, pedigrees, or family trees, were kept, and a number of registries developed to keep track of bloodlines. The Australian Shepherd Club of America (ASCA) was formed in 1957 to promote the breed, but several clubs continued to maintain registries for a number of years. A single breed standard was adopted in 1976, and the registries combined as ASCA in 1980. Some Aussies are registered with the National Stock Dog Registry (NSDR), which keeps a separate Australian Shepherd registry. The United States Australian Shepherd Association (USASA) was established in the early 1990s to represent the breed to the American Kennel Club (AKC). On September 1, 1991, the AKC recognized the Australian Shepherd breed and on January 1, 1993, accepted Aussies into the Herding Group. The Aussie is registered and shown in Canada under both ASCA and Canadian Kennel Club (CKC) rules and is now shown under various registries throughout the world. In the UK, the Aussie is currently on the import register at The Kennel Club; 68 were registered in 1998. Today's Australian Shepherd is even making his mark in the land down-under for which he was named.

The Australian Shepherd Breed Standard

A breed standard is a document created by members of a breed club to establish a set of characteristics that define a breed. In the US, the Australian Shepherd competes in shows sanctioned by several registries, the major ones being ASCA and the AKC. The ASCA and AKC breed standards differ somewhat, with the AKC standard allowing some traits that are considered faults by the ASCA standard. For instance, a level bite is considered a fault according to ASCA, but is acceptable in the AKC. So while a dog that meets the ASCA standard will also meet the AKC standard, the reverse is not necessarily true.

The following is the ASCA breed standard, which became effective January 15, 1977.

Slightly longer than tall, the Australian Shepherd is a well-balanced, solidly built dog of medium size and bone.

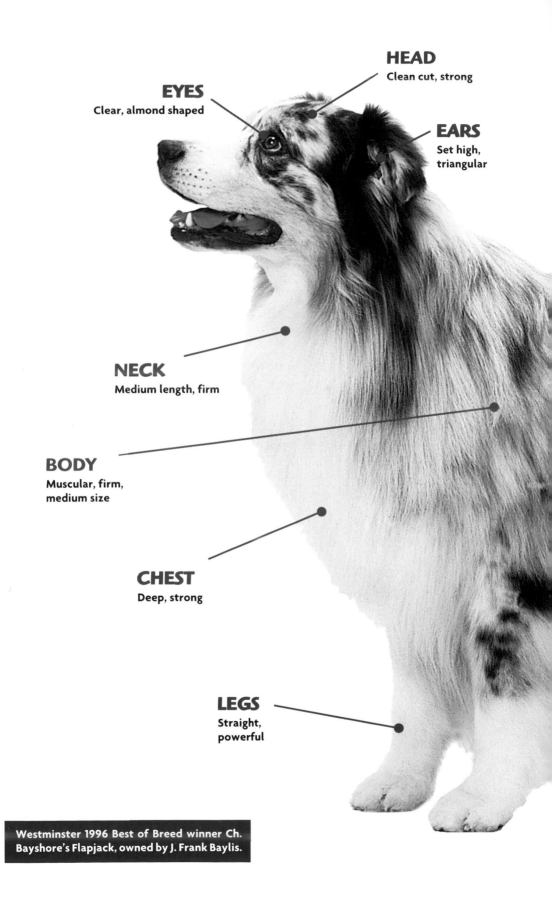

HEAD
Clean cut, strong

EYES
Clear, almond shaped

EARS
Set high,
triangular

NECK
Medium length, firm

BODY
Muscular, firm,
medium size

CHEST
Deep, strong

LEGS
Straight,
powerful

Westminster 1996 Best of Breed winner Ch.
Bayshore's Flapjack, owned by J. Frank Baylis.

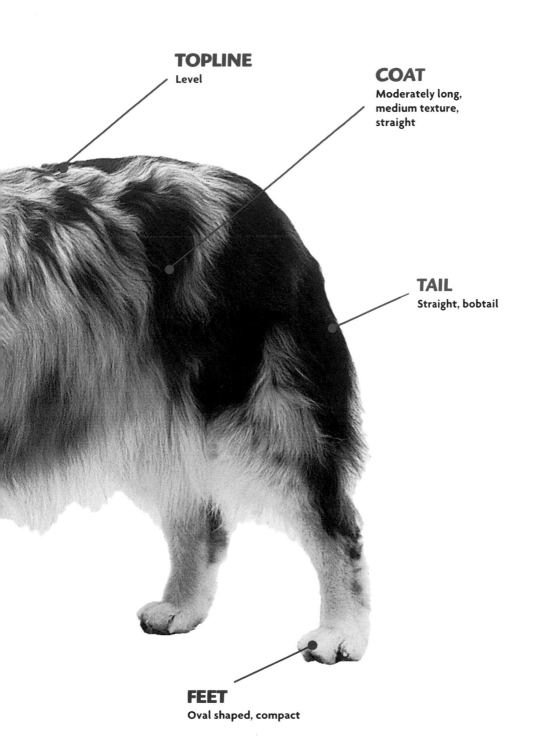

TOPLINE
Level

COAT
Moderately long,
medium texture,
straight

TAIL
Straight, bobtail

FEET
Oval shaped, compact

GENERAL APPEARANCE

The Australian Shepherd is a well-balanced dog of medium size and bone. He is attentive and animated, showing strength and stamina combined with unusual agility. Slightly longer than tall, he has a coat of moderate length and coarseness with coloring that offers variety and individuality in each specimen. An identifying characteristic is his natural or docked bobtail. In each sex, masculinity or femininity is well defined.

CHARACTER

The Australian Shepherd is intelligent, primarily a working dog of strong herding and guardian instincts. He is an exceptional companion. He is versatile and easily trained,

According to the standard, the Aussie has a clean-cut, strong head; expressive, almond-shaped eyes; and high-set, triangular ears.

performing his assigned tasks with great style and enthusiasm. He is reserved with strangers but does not exhibit shyness. Although an aggressive, authoritative worker, viciousness toward people or animals is intolerable.

HEAD

Clean-cut, strong, dry, and in proportion to the body. The topskull is flat to slightly rounded, its length and width each equal to the length of the muzzle which is in balance and proportioned to the rest of the head. The muzzle tapers slightly to a rounded tip. The stop is moderate but well-defined.

(A) Teeth

A full compliment of strong, white teeth meet in a scissors bite. An even bite is a fault. Teeth broken or missing by accident are not penalized.

Disqualifications: Undershot bites; overshot bites exceeding 1/8 inch.

(B) Eyes

Very expressive, showing attentiveness and intelligence. Clear, almond-shaped, and of moderate size, set a little obliquely, neither prominent nor sunken, with pupils dark, well defined, and perfectly positioned. Color is brown, blue, amber, or any variation or combination, including flecks and marbling.

(C) Ears

Set on high at the side of the head, triangular and slightly rounded at the tip, of moderate size with length measured by bringing the tip of the ear around to the inside corner of the eye. The ears, at full attention, break slightly forward and over from one-quarter (1/4) to one-half (1/2) above the base. Prick ears and hound-type ears are severe faults.

THE GUIDE TO OWNING AN AUSTRALIAN SHEPHERD

NECK AND BODY

The neck is firm, clean, and in proportion to the body. It is of medium length and slightly arched at the crest, setting well into the shoulders. The body is firm and muscular. The topline appears level at a natural four-square stance. The chest is deep and strong with ribs well-sprung. The loin is strong and broad when viewed from the top. The bottom line carries well back with a moderate tuck-up. The croup is moderately sloping, the ideal being thirty (30) degrees from the horizontal. Tail is straight, not to exceed four (4) inches, natural bobtail or docked.

FOREQUARTERS

The shoulder blades (scapula) are long and flat, close set at the withers, approximately two fingers width at a natural stance and are well laid back at an angle approximately forty-five (45) degrees to the ground. The upper arm (humerus) is attached at an approximate right angle to the shoulder line with forelegs dropping straight, perpendicular to the ground. The elbow joint is equidistant from the ground to the withers. The legs are straight and powerful. Pasterns are short, thick and strong, but still flexible, showing a slight angle when viewed from the side. Feet are oval shaped, compact, with close-knit, well-arched toes. Pads are thick and resilient; nails short and strong. Dewclaws may be removed.

HINDQUARTERS

Width of hindquarters approximately equal to the width of the forequarters at

Primarily a working dog of strong herding and guardian instincts, the Aussie is loyal, intelligent, versatile, and easily trained.

the shoulders. The angulation of the pelvis and upper thigh (femur) corresponds to the angulation of the shoulder blade and upper arm forming an approximate right angle. Stifles are clearly defined, hock joints moderately bent. The metatarsi are short, perpendicular to the ground and parallel to each other when viewed from the rear. Feet are oval shaped, compact, with close-knit, well-arched toes. Pads are thick and resilient; nails short and strong. Rear dewclaws are removed.

COAT

Of medium texture, straight to slightly wavy, weather resistant, of moderate length with an undercoat. The quantity of undercoat varies with climate. Hair is

The Australian Shepherd has a coat typical of a herding dog—one of moderate length and coarseness, with rich coloring that offers variety and individuality in each specimen.

short and smooth on the head, outside of ears, front of forelegs, and below the hocks. Backs of forelegs are moderately feathered; breeches are moderately full. There is a moderate mane and frill, more pronounced in dogs than bitches. Non-typical coats are severe faults.

COLOR

All colors are strong, clear, and rich. The recognized colors are blue merle, red (liver) merle, solid black, and solid red (liver) all with or without white markings and/or tan (copper) points with no order of preference. The blue merle and black have black pigmentation on nose, lips, and eye-rims. Reds and red merles have liver pigmentation on nose, lips, and eye rims. Butterfly nose should not be faulted under one year of age. On all colors the areas surrounding the ears and eyes are dominated by color other than white. The hairline of a white collar does not exceed the point at the withers.

DISQUALIFICATIONS

Other than recognized colors. White body splashes. Dudley nose.

GAIT

Smooth, free, and easy; exhibiting agility of movement with a well-balanced, ground-covering stride. Fore and hind legs move straight and parallel with the center line of the body; as speed increases, the feet, both front and rear, converge toward the center line of gravity of the dog, while the topline remains firm and level.

SIZE

Preferred height at the withers for males is 20 to 23 inches; that for females is 18 to 21 inches, however, quality is not to be sacrificed in favor of size.

Other Disqualifications:

Monorchidism (only one descended testicle) and cryptorchidism (undescended testicles).

An active dog with an even disposition, the Aussie is a good-natured and devoted canine companion. Story jumps for joy at a chance to play with her pal, Roger Boneham.

Characteristics of the Australian Shepherd

PHYSICAL TRAITS

A Coat of Many Colors

Look at a group of Aussies and you're likely to see a canine rainbow. Despite the limited number of colors that are permitted in the Aussie, the combinations that are possible with color and trim patterns make for infinite variety.

The Australian Shepherd comes in four acceptable colors: black, blue merle, red, and red merle. Genetically, blue merles are black and red merles are red. The merle gene modifies expression of the color gene by mixing lighter hairs with the main color. In blue merles, the merled areas of the coat are black and gray or silver; in red merles,

Among the Australian Shepherd's most prominent traits is his coat of many colors. Despite the limited number of colors permitted in the standard, the combinations possible with color and trim patterns make for infinite variety in the breed.

In blue merles, one of four acceptable coat colors, merled areas of the coat are black with gray or silver. A merle is produced when a genetic modification results in lighter hairs being mixed with the main color.

red and cream. Merles may also have patches of solid color. Some merle Aussies are nearly all merled, and some nearly all solid. Occasionally a dog has only a tiny bit of merling—sometimes on the tail, so it's gone once the tail is docked. Such a dog is a "cryptic" merle, and however much he appears not to be a merle, genetically he is.

Many Aussies also have white and/or copper (tan) markings. Copper is normally found trimming the cheeks, eyebrows, and legs. Some Aussies have "running copper," meaning copper on the top of the head or into the body. White is acceptable on the head, as long as both eyes are surrounded by color and both ears are colored. White is also acceptable on the ruff and chest, but must not extend farther back than the withers (the highest point of the shoulders). White stockings are also permitted.

Any of the four colors can occur without white or copper trim. A dog with no trim is known as "self colored," so a blue merle with no trim is a "self blue merle." White trim can occur without copper. In blacks and reds, this is called a "bi-colored" dog—a red with white trim but no copper is a "red bi." Copper can also occur without white. Finally, an Aussie of any color can have both white and copper trim. In blacks and reds, this is known as a "tri-colored" dog—"black tri" or "red tri."

Other colors do sometimes crop up, including sables, yellows, and blues (which look like faded black and are not merled). Unscrupulous people have been known to present such puppies as "rare colors" and try to sell them for more money. Don't buy it! They are "rare" because they are unacceptable in the breed. Such pups can

CHARACTERISTICS OF THE AUSTRALIAN SHEPHERD

A healthy "mismarked" puppy from a black tri dam and red merle sire. This black tri puppy does not meet the breed standard due to the white around his right eye, but he is a healthy puppy.

make fine pets, but they should not be bred and they are certainly not worth more money than a properly colored pup.

White Aussies

A white Australian Shepherd sounds like a beautiful animal. Why then are white Aussies disallowed by the breed standard? Because there are serious problems associated with *some* white Aussies.

A healthy merle Aussie is genetically *heterozygous* for merle; that is, his genes for that trait are not alike. The merle gene is dominant, so a dog with a merle gene is merle. A solid-color Aussie is *homozygous* for solid color; that is, his genes are alike for that trait. Solid color is recessive, so a solid dog has no gene for merle. A puppy inherits one gene from each parent for each trait.

When two healthy heterozygous merles are bred together, each can contribute either a merle gene or a non-merle gene to each pup. If each parent contributes a solid-color gene, the pup is a solid, not a merle. If one parent contributes solid and the other contributes merle, the pup is a heterozygous, or normal, merle.

If each parent contributes a merle gene, then the pup is a *homozygous* or *double* merle. Homozygous merle puppies are often mostly white, although not always. Sadly, they are nearly always blind or deaf or both.

Not all predominantly white puppies are homozygous merles. Some are *pattern whites*—they have white where they shouldn't, because the genes for white trim have gone overboard. Most pattern-white Aussies are healthy, but if the ear and area surrounding the ear is white, the dog may be partially or completely deaf. Pattern white dogs are not all merles; they can be solids as well.

If you are considering acquiring an Aussie with excessive white and are in doubt about his hearing, arrange for your veterinarian to administer a BAER test to determine how much, if any, hearing loss the dog has. Like all Aussies, an excessively white pup should also have his eyes examined by a veterinary ophthal—mologist.

Eye Colors

The Australian Shepherd can have eyes ranging in color from the darkest black-brown to amber to the palest icy blue. The color can vary from eye to eye and even within the eye. In merle Aussies, a flecked or marbled effect is quite common, with the colors swirled together. In solid (non-merle) Aussies, blue eyes also occur, as do partly blue eyes, but they are almost never flecked or marbled.

All eye colors are acceptable in all colors of Aussies. The blue eye in the Australian Shepherd is not linked to the genes that produce merle or those that produce white trim. Blue-eyed dogs are not "part albino." Blue eyes in non-merles are as healthy as any other eye color, are correct according to the breed standard, and do not indicate that the dog is a cryptic merle. There is no link between eye color and genetic eye disease.

PERSONALITY

The Australian Shepherd is a super high-energy, extremely intelligent dog. On the face of it, that sounds perfect—and in the right place, the Aussie is as perfect as a dog can be. In the wrong environment, the Aussie is a nightmare.

The Aussie's temperament is a direct result of his heritage. A working dog needs to follow direction, but also needs to think and act independently when necessary. He needs to be able to work long hours. He needs to be able to solve problems. The great intelligence of these dogs, which is necessary to out-think and control livestock, can be a problem when left ignored and unused. The Aussie needs

All eye colors are acceptable in all colors of Aussies, ranging from darkest brown to palest icy blue.

Like all smart and active dogs, an Aussie requires daily activity that will stimulate both mind and body. Callie, a FEMA certified rescue dog, uses her natural skills to do service work.

something to do with his mind as well as his body.

Many Aussies still work in traditional roles as stock dogs. Others are successful assistance and search and rescue dogs. For the pet Aussie, "jobs" can include obedience, agility, or tracking just for fun or for competition, learning tricks to entertain you and your friends, retrieving the morning paper or your slippers, performing therapy work—anything that requires mental focus and physical activity. If his owner fails to provide interesting activities, the Aussie will find his own entertainment, and his owner may not like it!

Working and show Australian Shepherds share many traits because they descend from the same foundation ancestors, but there are differences. The breed standard states that the Australian Shepherd is first and foremost a working dog with strong herding and guarding instincts. The intensity of those traits does vary throughout the breed, however. Aussies that are bred primarily to work stock usually have very high drive and stamina and are too intense for most pet owners. Potential Aussie owners should be open about their experience, expectations, and lifestyles. Responsible breeders will tell you if they think their own dogs are not suited to your needs.

Aussie puppies, like all puppies, are playful and can be destructive, especially when they are teething. But once past puppyhood, the Aussie is usually a responsible dog,

THE GUIDE TO OWNING AN AUSTRALIAN SHEPHERD

although most remain playful throughout their lives. With people they know and like, Aussies are extremely affectionate. Although well-bred Aussies are not by nature aggressive, they are naturally devoted to their families and protective of their homes and all who live there. The breed standard specifies that the Aussie should be reserved, which means he will take some time to size up new people before letting them "get familiar." In reality, there is a wide continuum of behaviors among Aussies, ranging from "never met a stranger" friendliness to extreme shyness or aggressiveness. Neither extreme is desirable, but the former "fault" is more livable in a pet.

When threatened, most Aussies will defend their territory and their pack—meaning your home and family. If you train and socialize your dog properly, he will be a reliable companion and defender. If you fail to train and socialize him and to assert yourself as his leader, he could become a liability.

Aussies can be wonderful companions for children, but they must be taught from the beginning that the children are their social superiors. Aussies that are raised with cats are usually fine with them, but some Aussies are cat aggressive. Like most herding dogs, Aussies tend to have a high prey drive and may chase animals, children, bicycles, and cars if not controlled. They need to have a fenced yard and to be on leash when out of their home and yard.

Like all smart, active dogs, Aussies need to learn to respect their owners and obey commands. This is not to say that an Aussie should be bullied; on the contrary, most Aussies want to please their owners and are devastated by emotional abuse. Obedience training using positive methods will build confidence in a "soft" or sensitive dog and ensure that a more confident or pushy dog knows who really is in charge. The most loving thing you can do for your Aussie is to train him so that he understands what you expect from him.

Australian Shepherds are sensitive, social animals. Perhaps the most endearing thing about Aussies to the people who love them is their devotion. An Aussie will follow his person to the ends of the earth—or the front door, the bathroom, the kitchen, the garage—everywhere he can! Sentencing an Aussie to a lonely life in the backyard is not only cruel, but will usually result in a variety of behavior problems, including barking, digging, jumping, and sometimes aggression. The best companions are the Aussies that live as part of the family.

Aussie puppies need extensive socialization through safe exposure to many different people, animals, and situations. Without this vital social education, the Aussie's natural guarding instincts can become overpowering for the dog, and he may respond with fearfulness or aggression, or a combination of the two. Aussies typically live 10 to 15 years, and they deserve to have the training and care needed to make those years happy ones for everyone involved.

IS THE AUSTRALIAN SHEPHERD THE RIGHT DOG FOR YOU?

Before acquiring an Australian Shepherd, think carefully about what it means to live with a highly intelligent, high-energy companion. Commitment to a dog means commitment to the whole dog, and it's important not to let a breed's virtues blind you to its challenges. For the right person, an Aussie is a delight. Who is the right person? The right Aussie owner is one who is committed to channeling the Aussie's tremendous energy and intelligence through exercise and training; one who is prepared to give the Aussie lots of the attention and affection that he craves and will return ten-fold; and one who doesn't mind being followed by a dog from room to room and beyond, if allowed. Before you decide that the Aussie is the right dog for you, please be sure you are the right person for an Aussie.

Australian Shepherds are naturally devoted to their families and protective of their homes. They can be wonderful companions for children.

THE GUIDE TO OWNING AN AUSTRALIAN SHEPHERD

The right Aussie owner is one who is committed to channeling his tremendous energy and intelligence through exercise and training—and one who is prepared to give and receive lots of affection!

CHARACTERISTICS OF THE AUSTRALIAN SHEPHERD

Finding Your Australian Shepherd

Once you have decided that an Aussie will fit in with your lifestyle, you still have some decisions to make. The first is whether to get a puppy or an adult. Many people never consider the possibility of taking an adult dog into their homes, but often a puppy is not the best choice. Puppies are babies. They have accidents on carpets. They have boundless energy. They need lots of attention. They are cute as can be, but the round little ball-of-fluff stage lasts a very short time. Then they turn into gawky, long-legged adolescents, and they stay that way for months. If you and your family can devote the time and energy it takes to raising a puppy, then a carefully bred Aussie pup may fit the bill. If not, consider adopting an adult from Aussie rescue or from a breeder. You will still have years of companionship and fun, but without the worries and work of bringing up a baby. Whether you decide on a youngster or an adult, please get your Aussie from a responsible source. Let's look at the options.

When you are ready to bring home an Australian Shepherd, be sure to purchase him from a responsible source. The puppy you choose should be bright-eyed, healthy, and responsive. This four-week old puppy won't be ready to go to his new home for several more weeks.

WHERE *NOT* TO GET YOUR DOG

Unfortunately, some unscrupulous people have hopped onto the bandwagon of sudden popularity for this beautiful breed. Some of them act out of ignorance. They know very little about genetics, and they

Puppy or adult? A bit of planning and research will help you to select an Aussie that fits in well with your family and lifestyle.

breed their bitch to the nearest available male with no thought to whether the two animals suit one another and are likely to produce sound puppies. The owner of the stud dog is probably cut from the same fabric because responsible stud dog owners do not stand their dogs to just any bitch. Sometimes a litter of acceptable pets is produced. More often, the puppies develop into dogs with mental and/or physical problems that cost their owners a great deal of money and heartache.

Worse yet are those who produce dogs strictly for profit. These "puppy millers" or "puppy farmers" care little for their dogs' physical and emotional needs as long as they continue to reproduce. When they are too worn out for that, they are disposed of. Puppy mill animals are not screened for genetic disease. Their nutrition is substandard, which hurts the pups as well as the dam. Puppies from puppy mills are often ill, infested with parasites, and undersocialized.

What about pet stores? *No responsible breeder ever sells puppies through a pet store.* Some stores will try to tell you otherwise, but the fact is that responsible breeders do not entrust the fate of their puppies to wholesalers and retailers in the pet industry. Most puppies in pet stores come from puppy mills or from backyard breeders. To get the puppies into the store at the "cute" age, they are removed from their mothers and siblings at four to five weeks of age—far too young for proper social development.

Remember that this little bundle of fluff is going to grow into a dog, and that dog will hopefully be with you for a long time. By

Responsible breeders ensure that good health and temperament are passed down to each succeeding generation. These adorable four-week-old Aussie puppies are owned by author and breeder Sheila Boneham.

THE GUIDE TO OWNING AN AUSTRALIAN SHEPHERD

Don't be surprised if a breeder asks you as many questions as you ask her—by answering her questions honestly, she can help you to select the puppy that suits you best.

buying an irresponsibly bred puppy, you may save one life, but you perpetuate the market that supports irresponsible breeding. Unwary buyers who purchase puppies from pet stores, puppy mills, and uninformed puppy producers often end up with Aussies displaying serious problems, including blindness, deafness, hip dysplasia, other health problems, and aggression—problems that responsible breeders work hard to prevent.

RESPONSIBLE BREEDERS

What to Look for in a Breeder

Responsible breeders are busy people. Most have several dogs to clean up after, groom, train, exercise, and play with. Most breeders also have human families, jobs, and other obligations. Their breeding activities are conducted as a hobby, not a business. Breeders are often gone on weekends to participate with their dogs in various kinds of training or competition. Don't be offended if the breeder asks you to call again later or doesn't return your call for a few days.

It's a good idea to have some questions ready, but you can often learn as much by letting someone simply talk. If you feel uneasy talking to a particular breeder, thank her for her time and go to the next name on your list. Make sure you feel comfortable with the breeder; you should be starting a long-term relationship, not just concluding a business transaction.

Start with general information. Ask how long the breeder has been in this breed and how many litters she has bred. Don't shy away automatically if it's her first litter—everyone starts somewhere, and some beginning breeders are well informed and very responsible. On the other hand, beware of the breeder who has bred several other breeds, jumped from breed to breed, or otherwise demonstrated lack of commitment to developing a quality line of dogs.

Find out what the breeder's goals are: Does she want to produce top-notch show dogs or athletic, highly trainable Aussies that will excel in obedience and agility? Does she breed to retain the traits for which the Aussie was developed? Is she striving to produce a versatile Aussie that will perform well in all arenas? Any of these are worthy goals, although you should consider whether dogs bred for a specific purpose will suit your needs best. If the breeder seems to have no clear goals or if her goal is "to make money," look for someone else.

Ask the breeder about her dogs' bloodlines. Even if it all sounds like gibberish to you, the answer will tell you about the breeder. Serious breeders know their dogs' pedigrees well and can recite them from memory. If the breeder doesn't seem to know the canine family tree, chances are she's not serious about producing high-quality dogs.

What does all this have to do with finding "just a pet"? Being a good pet is the most important thing a dog can do, and producing fine companions is not easy. Even in a carefully planned litter from champion parents and grandparents, there will be puppies that will not have what it takes to be competitive. Often the "fault" is very minor, and most people won't see it even if the breeder points it out. The pet puppies from a quality litter will be healthier, better tempered, and more beautiful than the best puppy from a poor-quality breeding. A responsible breeder will be committed to finding the right puppy—the one with the personality traits best suited to your needs in a canine companion.

How to Find a Responsible Breeder

How do you find one of these responsible breeders? Start with your local kennel club or Aussie club. The Australian Shepherd Club of America (ASCA) and the United States Australian Shepherd Association (USASA) maintain lists of member breeders and can also direct you to the club or clubs nearest to you.

The newspaper may lead you to a well-bred puppy. Dog magazines also list breeders, but keep in mind that some very appealing ads are placed by puppy mill operations. Be cautious, ask questions, and be prepared to walk away without a puppy if the breeder and the dogs don't measure up.

If you see an Aussie you like, find out where it came from. Find out if the owner is happy with the dog, and if they would go back for another. If that breeder doesn't have a puppy for you, she may be able to refer you to someone with similar lines.

Dog shows and obedience, agility, and herding trials can also be good places to meet breeders and owners and to see lots of dogs. Don't expect exhibitors to stop their preparations to talk to you—they are getting their dogs ready for competition and are under a good deal of stress. Buy a

THE GUIDE TO OWNING AN AUSTRALIAN SHEPHERD

Attending a dog show in your area is a good way to get information and breeder referrals from Aussie experts and owners.

catalog, watch the dogs, and enjoy the show! You can always ask for their name and phone number after they have competed.

The Internet is also a good tool for locating breeders. Aussie chat lists can lead you to breeders and give you a chance to size them up from what they write. Web sites, too, can lead you to your dream dog. But like all advertising, web sites can be misleading, so no matter how gorgeous the dogs and appealing the information, check out all claims.

When you have narrowed your options to two or three breeders, arrange to visit them if you live within visiting distance. (Please don't go directly from one breeder's place to the next, though—you could inadvertently spread disease between

kennels.) Are the facilities clean? Do the dogs appear to be healthy and clean? Do they have access to fresh water and room to move around and play? Are the dogs reasonably friendly? Does the breeder know every dog by name and know each puppy as an individual? The answer to each of these questions should be a resounding "yes."

You should be able to meet the mother unless the puppies are very young. Don't expect her to look her best while she's nursing, but do pay attention to her temperament, keeping in mind that it is normal for a bitch to be protective of her babies. If the sire is on the property, you should be able to meet him as well. Often the sire is not present, since serious breeders often breed their females to stud dogs owned by other people. You should be able to see pictures of the sire, though. If you don't like the parents, don't buy the puppy! Also ask if there are other relatives available for you to meet. If there are, you'll get a better idea of the looks and temperaments of the whole family.

If you haven't already done so, look at the paperwork on the parents and litter. First, be aware that registration does not indicate quality in the breeding dogs or the puppies. It merely shows that the parents of the puppies are registered, and that they are purebred as far as the registry knows. The breeder should show you the parents' registration papers, and the individual registration applications for the puppies or a copy of the litter registration if the individual applications aren't back from ASCA and the AKC yet. The breeder should give you a copy of the litter's pedigree, or family tree, showing four or five generations. Look for initials indicating titles earned in competition. In the US, at least half the dogs in the first two generations (the puppies' parents and grandparents) should have titles or be on their way to titles. Why? Because serious breeders are active in competition. Many puppy mill and pet puppies have champions back several generations and are advertised as "champion bloodlines," but the most important ancestors in terms of inheritance are the parents and grandparents.

You should also see proof that the parents have been certified free of genetic disease. Such certification includes at least Orthopedic Foundation for Animals (OFA) Hip or Pennsylvania Hip Improvement Program (PennHIP) certification and proof of annual eye clearance by a veterinary ophthalmologist. In the UK, certification is run by The Kennel Club and The British Veterinary Association (The BVA/KC Hip

If possible, try to see the parents of the pup you are considering. Their overall health and temperament will indicate what your Aussie will be like as an adult. This pup will hopefully be a gentle dog like his sire, shown here.

THE GUIDE TO OWNING AN AUSTRALIAN SHEPHERD

Dysplasia Scheme). Some breeders also have their dogs tested for thyroid function, healthy hearts, and elbow dysplasia.

Now the big question—how much? Of course, price is important, but don't sacrifice quality to price. You'll get no bargain doing that! In the long run, you are better off paying more for a puppy that has been carefully bred and raised and that is backed by a good contract signed by a responsible breeder than you are paying less for a lesser quality pup. Prices vary around the country, but you should expect to pay anywhere from a few hundred up to a thousand dollars for an Aussie pup from a reputable breeder, depending on whether you want competition quality or a pet with fewer guarantees.

Money alone won't clinch the sale with a responsible breeder. You will be required to sign a contract designed to protect the breeder, the buyer, and especially the puppy. The contract should give you at least 48 hours to have the puppy examined by a veterinarian and to return him for a full refund if he is not in good health. The contract should also cover genetic health. No one can guarantee that a puppy will not inherit a genetic problem, but responsible breeders offer compensation to the buyer in that event. Some breeders may offer to refund the purchase price or offer another dog in exchange. Be sure that you are satisfied with the terms of the guarantee.

If you are purchasing a pet in the US, expect to see a clause requiring you to have the dog altered and prohibiting you from breeding him or her. Such a requirement demonstrates a commitment to high breeding standards

When you purchase a purebred puppy, the breeder should supply you with three important documents: a health record containing an inoculation list, a copy of the dog's pedigree, and the registration certificate.

for Aussies and shows concern for keeping puppies out of the hands of irresponsible breeders. Be suspicious of any breeder who shows no interest in whether or not her puppies will be used for breeding.

A responsible breeder will take the puppy back at any time in his life, and many require that you give them the opportunity to do so before you place the puppy anywhere else. Of course, the breeder prefers to place each puppy in a good lifelong home and therefore will have lots of questions for you. If the breeder does not ask you for any information except your credit card number, go somewhere else.

If you think an adult Aussie may fit into your life better than a young puppy, you have two possibilities. One is, again, to find a responsible breeder. Breeders occasionally have older dogs to place in new homes. Sometimes a show-prospect puppy doesn't fulfill his early promise as far as competition. Sometimes a more mature dog is retired from showing or breeding, and the breeder decides that the dog would be happier living as someone's pet rather than staying with the breeder as one of a number of dogs. Occasionally, a breeder has a dog come back because of some problem in his new home— divorce, illness, or death, for instance. Such dogs are sometimes available at a nominal fee—perhaps the cost of altering.

Unfortunately, some Aussies find themselves the unwitting victims of their breed's many virtues. The fact is that no breed of dog is appropriate for every dog owner. Sadly, many people don't learn that until they have already acquired a dog. That's where Aussie rescue comes in.

RESCUED AUSSIES AS PETS

What is an Aussie Rescue?

"Rescue" refers to individuals and groups who take in, foster, and re-home dogs or other animals. Rescuers are unpaid volunteers who donate their time, dog-handling skills, and love. Two national organizations operate with local volunteers to help Aussies in need. These are the Australian Shepherd Rescue and Placement Helpline, Inc. (ARPH) and the Second Time Around Aussie Rescue, Inc. (STAAR).

From what do Aussies need to be rescued? Sometimes death or disablement of the owner or a serious change in personal or family circumstances displaces a dog. Sometimes dogs are found as strays and cannot be returned to their owners. Occasionally, legal action results in confiscation of dogs, and rescuers step in to help find them new homes. Some dogs are turned into rescues or shelters by owners who chose the breed without doing careful research first. Most dogs find themselves in the hands of rescuers due to human ignorance or laziness.

Although puppies occasionally come through rescue programs, most rescued Aussies are older adolescents or adults. Some (but not all!) have behavioral problems due to inadequate exercise, lack of training, or improper socialization. Such dogs were probably originally acquired by people with good intentions but bad dog-raising skills who discovered too late that love is not enough. Many rescued Aussies have no such problems, or their problems are so slight that they are easily correctable with training.

Most rescued dogs are fostered by a volunteer prior to placement. Fostering provides a "normal" setting in which to assess a dog's temperament, behavior, and level of training, which a kennel boarding arrangement cannot. Individual quirks can be identified so that each dog can be matched to an appropriate new home. All rescued dogs are altered. Aussies coming into rescue are often desperately in need of grooming, so that is done. Many are short on training, so rescuers provide some basic obedience

Consider adopting a well-socialized Aussie from a rescue group or shelter—the love and care you give will be returned ten-fold!

FINDING YOUR AUSTRALIAN SHEPHERD

Caring for a dog is a lifelong commitment, so make sure the decision to bring a puppy home is a carefully considered one.

and house manners. The health status of each rescued animal is checked, and although rescue programs often cannot afford to do everything that every dog needs, the new owners can be advised about possible problems.

ADOPTING A RESCUE DOG

Potential adopters fill out a detailed application form, provide references, and agree to a home visit by a rescue volunteer. Once an adopter is approved, the matching process begins, but it may take several weeks or even months to find the right dog. Patience is a virtue not only in owning a rescued Aussie, but in obtaining one as well.

Adoption fees range from under a hundred to several hundred dollars, depending on the dog's age, health status, veterinary care needed prior to placement (including spaying or neutering), and other factors. When a match is made, the adopter is required to sign an adoption contract. The adopter will also be given information about Aussies in general and his or her new Aussie in particular. Rescuers are usually more than willing to answer questions after the dog goes home, and all rescuers love to hear how well their former charges are doing in their new homes. That, after all, is what rescue is all about—placing dogs in need with the people who need them.

Feeding Your Australian Shepherd

CHOOSING A DOG FOOD

There is a mind-boggling choice of doggy diets available today, from cheap foods that are nutritionally questionable to high-priced "premium" foods to homemade and raw foods diets. We are bombarded with television and magazine advertisements for dog foods. No matter what you choose to feed your dog, someone will tell you what's wrong with that diet. The key to feeding your dog properly is a basic knowledge of canine nutritional needs, an ability to assess how your own dog is faring on the diet he gets, and willingness to look for nutritional solutions to problems such as dry skin or coat or lack of energy.

Aussie puppies should be fed puppy food until they are about four or five months old, then switched to adult maintenance food.

The amount of exercise your Australian Shepherd receives affects his food intake. A very active dog will require more to eat than a less active dog of the same size.

Most Aussie breeders recommend a high-quality, dry dog food. Aussie puppies should be fed puppy food until they are four or five months old, then switched to adult or maintenance food. Research shows that too much protein and calcium can contribute to skeletal and joint problems. Indeed, oversupplementation with vitamins, minerals, and other additives is a more serious problem for dogs in the US than malnutrition. Never add nutritional supplements to your puppy's or dog's diet without first consulting your veterinarian.

Another major problem for dogs today is obesity. For dogs, as for people, being overweight can contribute to many serious health problems and a shorter life. Individual animals, like individual people, require different amounts of food for optimum health and energy. How much food your puppy or dog requires will be influenced by several factors.

Activity Level

A dog that gets lots of running exercise or works all day will require more food than one with a less strenuous lifestyle.

Quality of Food

The caloric and nutritional values of commercial dog foods vary considerably. The more nutritionally dense the food, the less the animal needs to consume.

Genetic and Biological Variation

Every puppy and every dog is an individual. His genetic makeup will influence not only his physical characteristics, but also his metabolic efficiency. Two pups from the same litter can vary quite a bit in the amount of food they need to perform the same function under the same conditions.

COMPOSITION AND ROLE OF FOOD

The main ingredients of food are protein, fats, and carbohydrates. Food also contains vitamins, minerals, and water. Although all foods contain some of the basic ingredients needed for an animal to survive, they do not all contain those ingredients in the amounts or types needed by a specific type of animal. For example, many forms of protein are found in meats and plant matter. However, most plants contain "incomplete proteins" that lack certain amino acids that dogs require. Likewise, vitamins are found in meats and vegetation, but vegetables are a richer source of most vitamins than are meats. Vegetables are rich in carbohydrates, while meat is not.

Dogs are carnivores. The carnivore's tract has evolved to utilize the proteins in meat efficiently, but it is unable to break down the tough cellulose walls of plant matter. Therefore the carnivore eats all of its prey, including the partially digested food within the stomach. In commercially prepared dog foods, the cellulose in vegetables is broken down by heat as it cooks. However, cooking tends to destroy vitamins, so vitamins are added once the heat process has been

Your Australian Shepherd should have a healthy diet that includes the proper amount of proteins, fats, and carbohydrates.

The best way to determine if your puppy's diet is sufficient is by checking his bone and muscle development, his weight, and his level of activity.

completed. That's why it is important to feed a quality dog food to ensure complete nutrition for your dog.

Proteins are made from amino acids, of which at least ten are essential for health. The richest sources are meat, fish, poultry, milk, cheese, yogurt, fishmeal, and eggs. Vegetable matter that has a high protein content includes soybeans and dehydrated plant extracts. The actual protein content needed in your dog's diet will be determined by the activity level of the dog, his age, and the digestibility of the food.

Fats provide insulation against the cold and help cushion the internal organs. They provide energy and help transport vitamins and other nutrients, via the blood, to all the organs. Fat also makes food more palatable. Rich sources of fats are meats, milk, butter, and vegetable oils.

Although fat is essential in the diet, it should not be excessive. A high-fat diet will provide for the energy needs of the puppy, but it may not fulfill the pup's protein, vitamin, and mineral needs.

Vitamins are chemical compounds that help the body in many ways. Fruits are a rich source of vitamins, as is the liver of most animals. Many vitamins are unstable and easily destroyed by light, heat, moisture, or rancidity. Some vitamins, especially A and D, are toxic in excessive doses.

Minerals strengthen bone and cell tissue and assist in metabolic processes. As with vitamins, a mineral deficiency is most unlikely if you feed a good-quality diet, but too much can cause serious problems. Never add calcium or other minerals to a growing puppy's diet unless advised to do so by your veterinarian.

Water is essential to life and good health. Dogs get water directly from drinking and indirectly from metabolic water, that is, water released from food. A dog, like all animals, can tolerate a lack of food much longer than a lack of water. You may want to restrict late-night water intake while housebreaking a puppy, but otherwise a dog should have free access to clean water.

THE GUIDE TO OWNING AN AUSTRALIAN SHEPHERD

HOW MUCH SHOULD I FEED?

The best way to determine whether your pup or dog is getting the right amount of food is by observing his general health and physical appearance. If he is well covered with flesh, shows good bone development and muscle, is active as appropriate for his age, and is alert, then his diet is probably fine. An Aussie puppy will consume about twice as much as an adult. If you are getting a puppy, ask the breeder how much they feed their pups and use this as a starting point. If you are getting an adult, ask how much he is being fed, start there, and adjust for changes in food and exercise.

A healthy dog should eat his meal in about five minutes. If the dog quickly devours his food and is clearly still hungry, then he needs a bit more. If he eats readily but then begins to pick at it or walks away leaving a large quantity, then you are probably giving him too much. If, over a number of weeks, your Aussie starts to look fat, then he is obviously overeating; the reverse is true if he starts to look thin. To determine if your dog's weight is appropriate, run your fingers down the sides of his spine. You should be able to feel the ribs. If you are in doubt, ask your vet.

Use the manufacturer's recommend–ations for the amount to feed as a guideline only— the amount recommended on the bag is often considerably more than most dogs need, especially if the dog gets treats in addition to his regular meals.

Puppies from 8 to 16 weeks of age need three or four meals a day. Older puppies and dogs should be fed twice daily. Feeding times should be regular, especially while you are housetraining a puppy. The specific times you feed your Aussie don't matter, but keeping regular feeding times and feeding set amounts will help you monitor your puppy's or dog's health. If a dog that's normally enthusiastic about mealtimes suddenly shows a lack of interest in food, you'll know immediately that something is wrong.

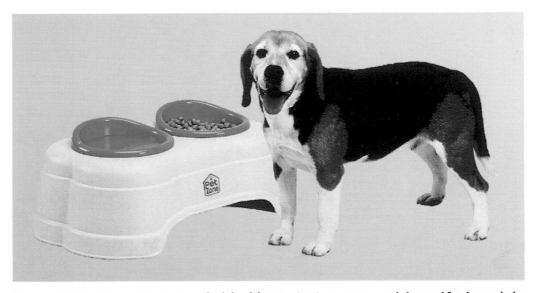

Proper nutrition is imperative to your dog's health. Veterinarians recommend elevated feeders to help reduce stress on your dog's neck and back muscles. Photo courtesy of Pet Zone Products, Ltd.

Grooming Your Australian Shepherd

All in all, the Australian Shepherd is an easy dog to keep looking good. Even if your Aussie will never see a show ring, he deserves regular grooming. You can learn to do the grooming, or you can take him to a professional groomer every six weeks or so for a complete "do." Even if you opt for the professional, though, you still need to groom your Aussie once or twice a week.

Mats can form almost overnight, particularly behind the ears and in the long hair of the front legs and the "pants," so

Keeping your pet well groomed is important to his health and well-being.

check on a daily basis. If you find a mat that you can't tease out with a comb or brush, you can remove it by making several cuts with a scissor through the mat and then brushing through it with a pin or slicker brush. Regular grooming will reveal foreign particles or parasitic pests hitching a ride, so you can remove them before they cause problems. You should also use your grooming sessions to check your dog for lumps or abrasions. If your dog has access to fields with foxtails or burrs, be sure to carefully inspect between the pads of the feet, in and behind the ears, under the elbows, and in the groin.

On the body, using a pin brush, bristle brush, or undercoat rake, separate small sections of hair and brush first in the direction of growth. Work your way from rear to head the entire length of the body. Be sure to part the hair to the skin and to brush through the hair, not just the surface of the coat. Surface brushing can leave mats close to the skin and lead to sores and infections. After all the hair is brushed, begin at the head and brush the hair forward to promote circulation. Then smooth it into place with a slicker brush. Brush carefully through the feathers on the legs.

Aussies do shed, and they "blow" their coats twice a year, in the spring and in the fall, when copious amounts of hair come out. Shedding is triggered by changes in the length of daylight, not temperature. House dogs shed year round because they live under artificially extended "daylight." During heavy shedding, loose hair can be

An Australian Shepherd does not require extensive grooming, but a thorough weekly brushing will keep his coat looking healthy and clean.

pulled out easily with a shedding rake, which has small teeth that grab the undercoat as you rake the coat.

Some people shave their Aussie in hot weather. Generally, that's not necessary and not a good idea. Many Aussies have light skin, and shaving can leave them vulnerable to sunburn. If an Aussie is kept properly brushed, he will usually do fine in all weather.

Trim the hair between the pads with blunt-nosed scissors and tidy up long hairs on the top of the foot for a neater appearance. Tails also need an occasional trim to remain tidy looking, and thinning out the hair around the anus helps keep that area clean. If possible, find a groomer or Aussie breeder or fancier who will help you the first few times.

Don't forget to keep your dog's nails trimmed. Dogs that walk on concrete

Regular grooming sessions combined with an all-over body check will help you to stay on top of your Aussie's physical condition.

sidewalks generally need their nails trimmed less frequently than those that run primarily on grass and carpets. However, when your dog walks on a hard surface and you hear "click click click"—it's time! Nails that are allowed to grow long prevent the foot from hitting the ground properly and can lead to problems. If your Aussie has dewclaws (the small toe on the inside of the leg above the foot), don't neglect them. Dewclaws can become ingrown if not kept trimmed.

Once a week, you also need to clean your Aussie's teeth and ears. You can purchase doggy dental kits from your veterinarian or at pet supply stores, or simply use baking soda on a damp cloth or toothbrush. Do not use toothpaste intended for people—dogs tend to swallow the toothpaste and it can make them sick. If you notice a buildup of tartar on your dog's teeth, ask your veterinarian or groomer to show you how to use a tooth scaler to remove it.

Clean your dog's outer ear canal about once a week with a cotton ball dipped in ear cleaner. You can use a commercial ear cleaner or make your own with one part rubbing alcohol and two parts white vinegar. Then dust with ear powder to dry the ear. Never insert any object into the ear; you can cause serious, permanent damage that way. If you notice a foul odor or brown discharge from the ear, have your vet check for ear infection.

Aussies do not generally develop a doggy smell if they are kept indoors and are brushed regularly, so frequent bathing usually isn't necessary. However, an occasional bath with a shampoo made for dogs is fine. Don't use human shampoos, because they will dry a dog's skin and coat. Shampoo diluted at a ratio of one part shampoo to two parts water will go on and rinse out more easily. Be sure to rinse your dog completely—soap left in the hair can cause irritation and skin sores.

Training Your Australian Shepherd

WHY TRAIN?

Every Aussie deserves to be trained to understand and obey your commands to come, to lie down, to stay, and to walk quietly at your side even in the presence of distractions. He also deserves to be taught the rules of the house. Is he allowed to beg for food when you are eating? Is he allowed on the furniture? May he jump up on you if you invite him? Be sure that you are the one who decides what is allowed and that you are consistent in enforcing the rules.

If possible, enroll your Aussie in a basic obedience course with a qualified instructor. Such classes usually meet once a week for eight to ten weeks. There are advantages of a training class over training alone at home. First, you make a commitment to train at a specific time. You will also have daily homework exercises, and in doggy school, everyone knows who did and didn't do their homework! Going to class is another opportunity for your dog to be socialized with other people and with all sorts of dogs. If you have a problem teaching your dog a certain command, your instructor can help you. Besides, it's lots of fun to have a weekly "date" with your dog and to spend time with other people who also enjoy spending time with their pets.

One of the main reasons people give up dogs is because of their own failure to train them. Dogs aren't born knowing what we want any more than children are; it's our responsibility to teach them.

SOCIALIZATION

The Australian Shepherd is not only an intelligent dog but generally an emotionally sensitive dog. It is extremely important to socialize an Aussie puppy; that is, to take him out into the world so that he can learn all about people and his environment. Puppies that are not given a chance to learn about the people, animals, and things around them may grow up to be fearful, even aggressive, adults.

Teaching your Australian Shepherd good manners and obedience skills will ensure that he will become a treasured member of the family for years to come.

THE GUIDE TO OWNING AN AUSTRALIAN SHEPHERD

As soon as your Aussie is old enough, take him with you wherever you go. Introducing him to new people, places, and experiences will help your puppy to become a confident and well-socialized adult.

The first few months of a puppy's life are a critical time for socialization. Unfortunately, these first months are also a time when your puppy is vulnerable to disease. However, if you take reasonable precautions, you can still get your puppy out to begin his education. Avoid high-risk environments, such as areas where stray or unvaccinated dogs may leave disease-carrying feces. Even if you have to carry him in some places, your pup may still meet people and see and hear lots of things.

Your puppy needs to meet all sorts of people—young and old, men and women, people of different races. A puppy that knows only a certain type of human being— say women or adults only—may show fear when exposed to men, children, or anyone different from what he knows. Fear can easily turn to aggression. Ask people who seem interested to pet your puppy gently and to give him a little treat (which you provide). Remember, never reward a fearful puppy with extra cuddling and cooing. Don't say, "It's OK," and pet him—what he'll understand is that "It's OK to be afraid and I will pet you for acting that way." Don't scold him, but do encourage him to be brave. When he accepts petting from a new person, that is the time to make a fuss over him.

If possible, enroll your pup in a puppy kindergarten class. These classes give the puppy a chance to interact with other puppies, as well as people. Look for a class that uses positive reinforcement instead of punishment. He's a baby, and he will make mistakes. Simply guide him to the correct behavior and reward him when he's right.

TRAINING YOUR AUSTRALIAN SHEPHERD

If you take your Aussie puppy to the same place to eliminate every time, he'll know what is expected of him. Reinforce what he has learned by praising him when he relieves himself in the correct area.

Socializing your puppy takes time and effort on your part, but it will pay off with a well-adjusted, confident companion of which you will be proud.

HOUSETRAINING

To most owners, housetraining is the first and most important kind of training that a puppy needs. If you are diligent about getting the puppy out to potty when he needs to go and patient when he does have an accident, housetraining your Aussie should go quickly and smoothly.

A puppy is able to control his bowels somewhat when he is a few months old, but he cannot control them fully until he is an adult. It's your job to anticipate his needs and be prepared for a few accidents. Expect your pup to need to urinate and defecate shortly after he wakes up from sleeping, shortly after eating, and after he has been playing awhile. If you take him out to his "place" immediately after he wakes up or

eats, he'll quickly learn to go outside to potty. When he's playing in the house, keep a close eye on him, and if he starts to sniff around, turn in circles, or arch his back slightly while walking, pick him up and take him out. If you want him to learn to use a particular part of the yard, take him there on leash and stay with him until he finishes. Soon he'll form the habit of going there and nowhere else, especially if you keep the area clear of feces. Remember that once a baby starts to go potty, he can't stop if he's on his own feet, so help him get to the right place. As he gets older and has more control, he'll be able to race out the door when you open it and do his business where you want him to. When he does relieve himself in the right place, praise him in a happy voice and pet him.

A word of caution: Puppies do have accidents, and adults who haven't taught their puppy where to go may have a few as well. Never punish a dog for an accident—don't rub his nose in it, hit him, or yell. Help him to make the right decisions and reward him for success. If your puppy or rescued dog isn't reliable in the house, don't leave him unsupervised. If he does have an accident, take him outside. Clean the spot with a good odor and stain remover (available at pet supply stores) so that it isn't "labeled" as a potty place. Most dogs prefer to keep their homes—their dens—clean, but they need some guidance to learn how.

UNDERSTANDING YOUR AUSSIE

As a new puppy or dog owner, you will inevitably get lots of advice from friends, neighbors, and relatives, some of whom may even know what they're talking about. Many, however, will not! You will also probably read articles and books about puppy and dog training. There are some excellent books available on the subject, and they don't all agree on the most effective methods. The truth is that dogs are not all alike and owners are not all alike, and what works for someone else and his dog may or may not work for you and yours. In the end, your dog's education, social adjustment, and life are in your hands. Keep an open mind, observe what works and what doesn't work with your dog, and let common sense prevail. There is no one way that is superior to all others, nor one dog that is an exact replica of another. Each is an individual. Your puppy may have limitations, but the single biggest limitation that most dogs face is their owners' inability to understand their needs and how to cope with them.

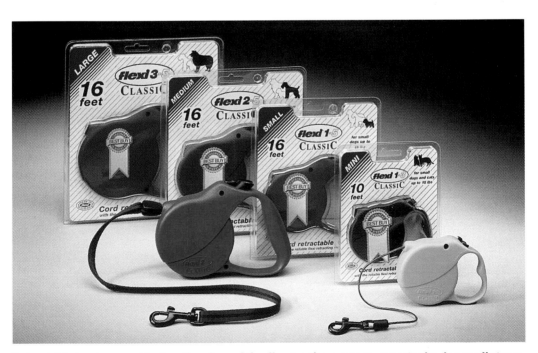

Retractable leashes provide dogs freedom while allowing the owner to restrain the dog at all times. Leashes are available in a wide variety of models for all breeds of dog. Photo courtesy of Flexi-USA, Inc.

TRAINING YOUR AUSTRALIAN SHEPHERD

Activities for the Australian Shepherd

The Australian Shepherd is truly a versatile breed. Aussies were bred to be all-around working ranch dogs, and the intelligence and athleticism needed to be successful in that environment are readily adaptable to other work and sports. Whether you are looking for a top-notch competitor or a buddy to join you for fun and games, an Aussie may fit the bill.

COMPETITIVE SPORTS

Herding

There's nothing quite like the thrill of seeing a dog's instinct kick in as he finds the activity he was bred for—and for Aussies, that is herding. Not all Aussies have what it takes to be truly competitive herding trial dogs, but most do have some instinct. The AKC, ASCA, and the American Herding

Versatile and athletic dogs, Australian Shepherds excel at a variety of activities when properly trained. This handsome Aussie masters the agility high jump with ease.

THE GUIDE TO OWNING AN AUSTRALIAN SHEPHERD

When competing in conformation events, your Australian Shepherd will be judged on how closely he conforms to the standard for the breed.

Breeds Association (AHBA) all offer herding tests and trials in which Aussies participate. If you'd like to try herding for fun or for competition, your local Aussie club can direct you to clinics and instructors in your area.

Agility

Agility is the fastest growing canine sport in the world, and Aussies excel at it. Agility requires the dog to negotiate jumps, tunnels, and other obstacles while the handler directs him around a course. You can do agility just for fun with simple homemade equipment, or you can join an agility class and eventually enter competition to earn titles.

Flyball

Flyball is another sport that really gets dogs excited. Dogs run relay races as teams. Each team member runs down a lane over a series of jumps, hits a peddle on a box to release a tennis ball, grabs the ball, and races back.

Obedience

Obedience training and competition is another sport at which Aussies do well. However, it is vital to realize that Aussies easily become bored, and you cannot drill an Aussie on an exercise. The top obedience Aussies are trained with fun and positive reinforcement and lots of variety in the training.

Tracking

Tracking is another activity where the dog just does what comes naturally, although you have to teach him to follow the track you show him. Your dog can earn tracking titles, or you can train him to track just for fun.

Whether you are looking for a top-notch competitor or a buddy to join you for fun and games, an Aussie may fit the bill.

Conformation

Conformation involves competition in which the dog is judged against the breed standard. The purpose of conformation is to assess the quality of potential breeding stock, so it is open only to intact animals. (In the UK, neutered animals are allowed to be shown providing that The Kennel Club is informed in advance about the operation.) ASCA has approved a conformation program for altered Aussies commencing in 2000. Conformation may look simple, but a lot of training and practice go into preparing a dog to look great in the show ring. Local kennel clubs often offer classes to help you prepare yourself and your dog for competition.

Freestyle

Musical freestyle, or heelwork to music, is a beautiful, fairly new sport that essentially amounts to dancing with your dog. It is obedience set to music, in which dog and handler perform a choreographed routine.

JUST FOR FUN

Hiking and backpacking are a lot more fun with a friend, and Aussies are naturals. Your dog can learn to wear a backpack (but build him up slowly to carrying weight). He can carry his own food and water, and if you help him a bit, he can be a good citizen and carry his feces back in a baggy for proper disposal so that public areas will continue to be open to well-mannered dogs and their responsible owners.

Jogging is a great way to keep you and your Aussie in shape. Before you start a jogging program, be sure that your dog's nails are trimmed, his pads are in good condition, and he's not overweight. Start slowly and build up gradually. If possible, jog mostly on soft surfaces like dirt trails or grass; pavement is harder on your dog's joints, and in the summer it can be very hot on his foot pads.

Swimming is great exercise for a dog, and most Aussies love the water. Be cautious about water containing chemicals, because many city parks and other sites treat their ponds to control algae, and dogs can become ill from swallowing the water or licking their coats. If your Aussie swims in your swimming pool (always with supervision), bathe him afterward to remove the chlorine from his coat.

THE GUIDE TO OWNING AN AUSTRALIAN SHEPHERD

Your Healthy Australian Shepherd

Dogs, like other animals, are susceptible to problems and diseases that would seem overwhelming if we listed them all. However, well-bred and well-cared-for animals are less prone to health problems than are carelessly bred and neglected animals. When a problem does arise, work closely with your veterinarian (not your friends and relatives!) to resolve it. This doesn't mean that a few old remedies aren't good standbys when all else fails, but in most cases, modern science provides the best treatments for disease.

PHYSICAL EXAMS

Your dog should receive regular physical

There are many parasites, like fleas and ticks, that your dog may encounter when playing outside. Be sure to check his coat thoroughly when he comes in from the outdoors.

As a responsible Australian Shepherd owner, you should have a basic understanding of the medical problems that affect the breed.

examinations. A new canine family member should visit your vet for a checkup within a few days of arriving home. If you have a puppy, he will make several more visits during the first months to complete his puppy vaccines. After that, your dog should be examined annually when he gets his vaccine boosters. Your vet should give the dog a thorough examination and check a fecal sample for intestinal parasites and a blood sample for heartworm infection.

You should also examine your dog every day or two at home. Doing so will often catch problems while they are small and easily treatable. Besides, puppies need lots of handling to become well socialized, and older dogs like the social interaction of being groomed and examined. Simply start at the dog's head and work your way back, gently feeling for anything unusual and looking for signs of parasites such as fleas and ticks. Dogs sometimes pick up thorns, burrs, and other sticky things that can cause serious problems if they work their way deeply into the flesh. Don't forget to check your dog's ears, the pads of his feet, and his belly and anal area.

EXTERNAL PARASITES

Fleas are small and very mobile insects. They may be red, black, or brown in color. The adults suck the blood of the host, while the larvae feed on the feces of the adults, which is rich in blood. Flea "dirt" (feces) is visible on the dog's skin as tiny clusters of blackish specks. If you moisten flea dirt slightly, it will turn red, because it consists primarily of blood. The eggs of fleas may be laid on the host animal, but usually they are laid off the host in a favorable place, such as the dog's bedding. They normally hatch in 4 to 21 days, depending on the temperature, but they can survive up to 18 months. Flea larva look like tiny maggots. The larva molt twice before forming a pupae, which can survive long periods until the temperature or the vibration of a nearby host causes them to emerge as full-fledged fleas.

Aside from being annoying pests, fleas carry tapeworm and disease. If they infest a host in large numbers, they can cause anemia. Some dogs are allergic to flea saliva and react to flea bites with frantic scratching and biting, resulting in open sores that can become infected.

Discuss your flea-control options with your veterinarian, who will be able to suggest the most effective strategy for flea control for your situation and area.

Ticks are arthropods (relatives of spiders). Most ticks are round and flat, and they have eight legs. Ticks that are gorged with blood from a host animal or gravid with eggs look like small beans with legs. The tick buries its head parts in the host and gorges on blood. Ticks are often picked up when dogs play in fields, but may also arrive in your yard via wild animals, birds, stray cats, or other dogs. Like fleas, ticks are not just annoying; they are carriers of disease.

The most troublesome type of tick is the deer tick that spreads Lyme disease, which can cripple a dog (or a person). Deer ticks are tiny and very hard to detect. Often by the time they're big enough to notice, they've been feeding on the dog for a few

The cat flea is the most common flea of dogs. It starts feeding soon after it makes contact with the dog.

days—long enough to do their damage. Your veterinarian can advise you of the danger of Lyme ticks in your area and may suggest your dog be vaccinated for Lyme disease. Always go over your dog's coat with a fine-toothed flea comb when you come home from walking through any area that may harbor deer ticks, and if your dog is acting unusually sluggish or has sore joints or muscles, seek veterinary advice.

Tick removal must be done carefully. It's very easy to pull the body off and leave the head in the host, which can lead to infection. In addition, squeezing a tick while attempting to remove it can force fluids from the tick into the host, increasing the risk of infection or disease. Special tick-removers are available in some pet supply stores. You can also remove a tick by dabbing it with a strong saline solution, iodine, or alcohol, which will make it loosen its grip, and then pulling it gently and carefully straight out with forceps, tweezers, or your fingers after placing a tissue over the tick. Check

the skin. You should see a small hole. If you see a black spot, you have left the head. Immediately clean the bite with alcohol or iodine, then wait five minutes and dab on antiseptic ointment. Wash your hands and any tool you used. If ticks are common in your area, ask your vet for a suitable pesticide to be used in kennels, on bedding, and on the puppy or dog.

Skin Problems

Several skin disorders can cause problems for dogs. These include fungal infections, such as ringworm, infestations of mites that cause mange, and a number of nonspecific problems lumped together as eczema.

Ringworm is not a worm but a highly contagious fungal infection. It usually appears as a sore-looking bald circle, but if your puppy or dog develops any form of bald patches, have your veterinarian check him. Fungal infections can be very difficult to treat and even more difficult to eradicate, and modern drugs are much more effective than home remedies. Be sure to dispose of all bedding used by an infected pet, preferably by burning. Ringworm can be spread among your pets, and it is one of the few diseases that can be transmitted by dogs to people. If your dog has ringworm, ask your vet for advice on preventing its spread in your household.

Mange is caused by various species of mites that feed on skin debris, the hair follicles, and tissue. Symptoms of mange include hair loss often followed by a flaky crust. Often dogs will scratch themselves and worsen the original condition by opening lesions that make viral, fungal, or parasitic attack easy. It is vital to determine the species of mite causing the problem in order to treat mange effectively. If you suspect that your dog has mange, have him examined by your vet.

Eczema is a nonspecific term applied to many skin disorders with diverse causes. Sunburn, chemicals, foods, drugs, pollens, even stress can all damage the skin and coat, resulting in itching, hair loss, and open sores. Given the range of causal factors, it is often difficult to determine the cause of eczema, which in turn makes effective treatment difficult. Once again, it is important to work closely with your veterinarian to diagnose and cure the problem.

INTERNAL DISORDERS

Some symptoms of illness, such as vomiting or diarrhea, may be nothing more than the result of your Aussie eating too much or becoming too excited. If symptoms continue for more than a few hours or if the dog exhibits more than one sign of illness, it is important to have an accurate diagnosis. The following symptoms, especially if they accompany each other or are progressively added to earlier symptoms, mean you should visit the veterinarian right away.

Continual Vomiting

All dogs vomit from time to time, and it is not necessarily a sign of illness. However, continual vomiting is a clear sign of a problem. It may indicate a blockage in the intestinal tract, it may be induced by worms, or it could be due to a number of diseases. If your dog vomits bright, fresh blood or partially digested blood, which looks like coffee grounds, get him to a vet as soon as possible.

Diarrhea

This too may be nothing more than a temporary condition due to many factors. A change of home, stress, a change in water, and a change in diet can induce diarrhea. If diarrhea persists more than 48 hours or if you see bright red or black blood in the feces, get your dog to the veterinarian as soon as possible.

Running Eyes and/or Nose

Occasionally, exposure to cold or dust will cause a dog's eyes to water or nose to run, and it is nothing to worry about. However, persistent watering eyes or runny nose may indicate something more serious.

Coughing

Prolonged coughing is a sign of a problem, usually of a respiratory nature,

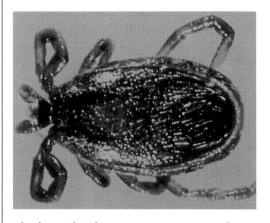

The deer tick is the most common carrier of Lyme disease. Photo courtesy of Virbac Laboratories, Inc., Fort Worth, Texas.

Regular physical examinations are vital to the health and long life of your canine companion.

THE GUIDE TO OWNING AN AUSTRALIAN SHEPHERD

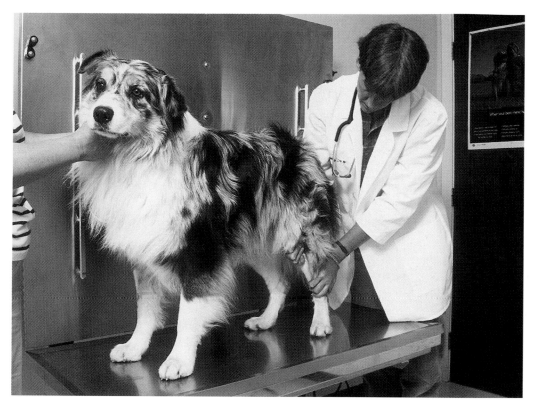

The importance of consulting a veterinarian on the diagnosis of internal disorders cannot be overemphasized—a relatively common problem could also be a sign of something more serious.

although it can also indicate other serious problems such as heartworm infection.

Crying

Continual crying may be only a minor, temporary problem, but it could be more serious. If it occurs more than once or if your dog cries when urinating or defecating, see your vet. At times, your dog may cry when touched. Obviously, if you handle a pup roughly, he might yelp. However, if he cries even when lifted gently, then he may have an internal or skeletal problem, which must be diagnosed.

Refuses Food

Generally puppies and dogs are greedy about food. Some might be a bit fussy, but none should refuse more than one meal. If they go for more than a day without showing any interest in food, then something is wrong and your veterinarian should be notified.

General Listlessness

All pups and dogs have off days when they don't seem their usual, happy selves. If such listlessness persists for more than two days, see your vet.

Intestinal Worms

There are many species of worms and a number of these live as parasites in dogs and other animals. Many create no problem at all, so you are not even aware that they exist. Others can be tolerated in small numbers, but become a major problem if they number more than a few. Puppies should have fecal exams when they get their vaccinations, and adult dogs should

All dogs have off days when they do not seem themselves. However, if this lethargic condition persists, you should have your Aussie examined by a professional.

have an annual fecal exam so that they can be treated if necessary. If you see evidence of worms in your dog's stools, take a specimen to your vet so that he can prescribe the appropriate wormer.

Roundworms

These may grow to a length of 8 inches (20 cm) and look like strings of spaghetti. The worms feed on the digesting food in the intestines. In chronic cases, an infected puppy will develop a pot-belly, have diarrhea, and vomit. For a while, he will always seem to be hungry, but eventually he will stop eating. Roundworms are common in puppies, and responsible breeders worm their bitches and puppies regularly to eliminate them. Roundworms can be passed to humans, so until your puppy is declared free of worms by your veterinarian, it's important to practice proper hygiene and teach children to do the same.

Tapeworms

These are difficult to diagnose from fecal specimens, but the worms shed segments, which look like rice and can be found sticking to the anus. Dogs acquire tapeworms by eating mice, fleas, rabbits, and other animals that serve as intermediate hosts. The dog must eat the host while the worms are in the larval form, after which the worms develop in the dog. Keeping your dog free of fleas will help prevent tapeworm.

Other Worms

Hookworms, whipworms, and thread–worms also affect puppies and dogs and cause problems including weight loss, anemia, respiratory infection, and diarrhea. Your dog's best protection against worms is your attention to cleanliness, your recognition of telltale symptoms, and regular veterinary examinations.

Heartworm

Heartworm disease is a problem in some places and practically nonexistent in other areas. Check with your vet about the need for heartworm prevention where you live. If you plan to travel with your dog, check before you go—your dog may need protection during your travels.

Heartworm larvae are carried from an infected dog to a new host by a mosquito. The larvae then travel to the host's heart, where they take up residence and grow. Eventually, they fill the heart sufficiently to cause congestive heart failure. Fortunately, heartworm is easy to prevent with daily or monthly preventive medication. As an added bonus, many heartworm preventatives also prevent intestinal parasites.

THE GUIDE TO OWNING AN AUSTRALIAN SHEPHERD

A word of caution: Ivermectin is used as the active ingredient in some heartworm preventatives. Aussies, like other collie-type breeds, can be sensitive to Ivermectin. Although manufacturers claim that the amount of Ivermectin in normal dosages of their medications will not hurt an Aussie, there is considerable anecdotal evidence from Aussie owners and breeders that prolonged usage can induce seizures in some dogs. There are effective heartworm preventatives that use other active ingredients, so please consider carefully whether it is worth the risk to give your dog a product containing Ivermectin.

VACCINATIONS

Every puppy and adult dog should be vaccinated against distemper, hepatitis, parainfluenza, canine parvovirus, and rabies. In fact, in most states the law requires all dogs be vaccinated against rabies either every year or every three years. Check with your veterinarian for

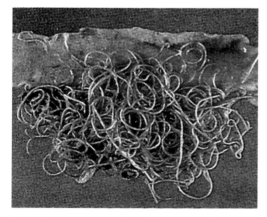

Roundworms are spaghetti-like worms that cause a pot-bellied appearance and dull coat, along with more severe symptoms, such as diarrhea and vomiting. Photo courtesy of Merck AgVet.

Whipworms are hard to find unless you strain your dog's feces, and this is best left to a veterinarian. Pictured here are adult whipworms.

the local requirements. There is some disagreement on the need for vaccinations against leptospirosis, bordatella (kennel cough), and coronavirus, so consult your vet for advice for your area and situation. When you bring your puppy home, be sure to get a record of the vaccines your puppy or dog has received already.

The age at which vaccinations are given can vary, but generally puppies get their first shots at five to six weeks of age and boosters at three- to four-week intervals for three or four sets. Initial rabies vaccinations are usually given between three and six months. (In the UK, rabies vaccinatins are not given.) The vaccines "teach" the puppy's immune system to recognize harmful bacteria and viruses and attack them. Annual booster shots ensure that the immune system doesn't "forget" what the enemy looks like. If a vaccinated puppy or dog is exposed to disease, his immune system is able to respond before the animal becomes ill. Immunization is not 100 percent effective, but it comes very close.

Rely on your veterinarian for the most effectual vaccination schedule for your Aussie puppy.

Certainly it is better than giving the animal no protection.

ACCIDENTS

Puppies and dogs, like children, play hard and go through clumsy periods, and they get their share of bumps and bruises. Most heal in a few days. Small cuts should be cleaned with hydrogen peroxide or alcohol and then smeared with an antiseptic ointment. If a cut looks more serious, do your best to stop the blood flow with direct pressure and take the pup to a veterinarian. Never apply a tourniquet or excessive pressure that might restrict the flow of blood to the limb.

If your dog is burned, apply cold water or an ice pack to the surface to stop further tissue damage. If it is a chemical burn, wash away the offending substance with copious amounts of water and be careful not to burn yourself in the process. Never apply petroleum jelly, butter, vegetable oil, or similar substances to a burn—they can cause infection. Trim away the hair if need be. If the burn is severe, there is danger of shock, so it is vital that you get your dog to a veterinarian as quickly as possible.

If you think your dog has broken a bone, try to keep him as still as possible. Wrap him in a blanket to restrict movement. If

THE GUIDE TO OWNING AN AUSTRALIAN SHEPHERD

possible, make a stretcher out of a board or blanket and get some help to lift the dog into a vehicle for transport to the veterinarian.

If your dog has an accident in which internal injuries are likely, such as being struck by a car or falling from some height, try to restrict movement. Keep the head from tilting backward to reduce the risk of choking. Keep him warm and get him to a vet immediately.

SPECIAL BREED CONCERNS

Overall, the Australian Shepherd is a healthy breed, but like all living things, it is subject to some hereditary diseases. The most common genetic health problems in the breed are inherited hip dysplasia and eye defects. Deafness, heart disease, and epilepsy also occur in the breed.

Canine Hip Dysplasia

Canine hip dysplasia, or CHD, is a serious, potentially crippling condition in which the bones that make up the hip joint are malformed and do not fit together properly. This poor fit makes the dog prone to development of painful arthritis. CHD is an inherited condition. You cannot tell if a dog has CHD by watching him move, so it is vital that all Australian Shepherds used for

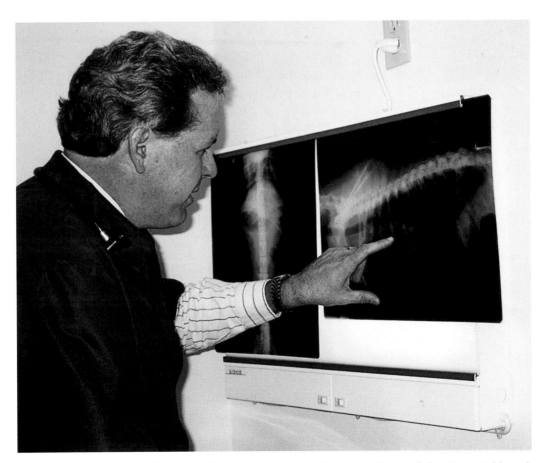

If your Australian Shepherd becomes ill or sustains an injury from an accident or fall, acting quickly and appropriately can save his life. For example, it is a good idea to x-ray any dog hit by a car.

Although the Australian Shepherd is essentially a very healthy breed, it's important to be aware of breed-specific health concerns and hereditary diseases.

breeding be x-rayed by a qualified radiologist or orthopedic specialist and found to be free of hip dysplasia.

The Orthopedic Foundation for Animals (OFA) rates the structure of hips by evaluating x-rays. To be certified, the dog must be at least 24 months old when x-rayed. (In the UK, under the BVA/KC Hip Dyslpasia Scheme, the dog must be at least 12 months old when x-rayed.) Dogs that are considered free of CHD are rated Excellent, Good, or Fair. Dysplasia is also ranked at three levels of severity. Of more than 13,385 Aussies checked by OFA, 6.2 percent have hip dysplasia. Chances are that the actual incidence of CHD is higher than that, because very often x-rays that clearly show poor hip structure are not sent to OFA, and irresponsible breeders don't have their dogs checked.

The Pennsylvania Hip Improvement Program (PennHIP) uses a different evaluation method that can be applied to puppies as young as four months. PennHIP provides two numbers. First, they provide a "distraction index" for each hip independently. That index indicates the laxity or looseness of the hip joint. Laxity has been found to be an accurate predictor of degenerative joint disease. Second, PennHIP provides a percentile score that indicates where an individual dog stands in relation to all members of his breed that have been evaluated by PennHIP. The percentile ranking can change as more dogs are tested, but the laxity index will not.

Some Aussie breeders are now using PennHIP. Most use OFA, and some use both systems. It doesn't really matter which system is used on an individual dog, as long as the hips are evaluated and found to be normal prior to breeding.

Genetic Eye Disease

Aussies are prone to several genetic eye diseases. Breeders should have all breeding animals certified free of disease annually until they are at least nine years old by a veterinary ophthalmologist—a regular vet is not trained and does not have the equipment to do this examination. Puppies, too, should have their eyes checked by a veterinary ophthalmologist at around seven weeks of age. Buyers should insist on seeing the paperwork before buying a puppy.

Merle ocular dysgenesis occurs only in homozygous or "double" merles; that is, puppies that inherit two merle genes in a merle-to-merle breeding. Often these pups have a lot of white on their heads and bodies, but not always, and not all Aussies with white on their heads and bodies are homozygous merles. If you are looking at

Aussies are prone to several genetic eye diseases, so have your puppy's eyes checked by a veterinary ophthalmologist at around seven weeks of age.

an Aussie with white on the ears, around the eyes, or on the main part of the body, find out what color the parents are. If they are both merles, insist on eye and hearing examinations before you buy a merle puppy.

Dogs affected with merle ocular dysgenesis have some combination of the following conditions: microphthalmia (a small eyeball); eccentric pupils (pupils that are not centered); coloboma or other irregularities of the iris; lens luxation; cataract; retinal dysplasia or detachment; persistent pupillary membrane; equatorial staphyloma; and lack of a tapetum (the "reflector" in the back of the eye that collects light, and makes dogs' eyes glow when light hits them).

A cataract, or an opacitiy on the lens of the eye, is the most common eye disease in Australian Shepherds. Not all cataracts are inherited; they can be caused by injury, other diseases, and old age. Nevertheless,

It is very important that the veterinarian you choose is familiar with Australian Shepherds and the problems that the breed can experience.

genetically acquired cataracts are a serious problem in the breed. Hereditary cataracts, usually referred to in Aussies as "juvenile cataracts," are bilateral, meaning they occur in both eyes, although they don't always become evident at the same time. If a cataract is discovered on one eye, the dog should be checked again in six months to see if a cataract is forming in the other eye. Genetic cataracts are "progressive," starting small and slowly growing until the entire lens is clouded and the dog is virtually blind. Cataracts are not painful, and they usually develop slowly enough so that the dog and his owner have time to adjust to his loss of vision. In Aussies, juvenile cataracts usually first become apparent when the dog is between one and a half and three years of age, although they may appear as late as seven years of age. Juvenile cataracts are difficult to eliminate, in part because of this wide range of initial onset. Very often, by the time dog is diagnosed with the disease, he or she has already produced puppies. In addition, the mode of inheritance of juvenile cataracts is still unknown.

Collie Eye Anomaly (CEA) is actually a complex of defects including choroidal hypoplasia, optic disc coloboma/staphyloma, and retinal detachment. The defects may differ in the two eyes, but both will be affected. CEA is not linked to coat or eye color, nor does it cause pain or discomfort. Some affected dogs are blind in one or both eyes, but most are not and they can live happy, normal lives; however, they should not be bred.

CEA is present at birth and is not progressive. Puppies with CEA show no outward symptoms, and the condition can only be detected by a veterinary ophthalmologist using special instruments. Some CEA puppies "go normal" after eight to ten weeks of age, meaning that they appear to be normal. However, since CEA is recessive, an affected dog still has two defective genes. All of their offspring will be carriers of CEA, and those that inherit the gene from the other parent as well will be affected. Therefore, it is important that puppies be examined by a veterinary ophthalmologist between six and eight weeks.

Iris coloboma is a condition in which part of the iris is missing. A small coloboma will not affect a dog's vision, but a large one will render the iris incapable of contracting to reduce the amount of light entering the eye. A dog with a large iris coloboma will squint in bright light, possibly causing him some discomfort and reduced vision. Dogs that are affected with iris colobomas or that produce them in their puppies when bred to different mates should not be bred.

Persistent pupilary membrane (PPM) is the remains of the "pupilary membrane" that covers the eye in a fetus prior to birth. The membrane is supposed to "resolve" or disappear shortly after birth, before the puppy opens his eyes. Sometimes it does not disappear on schedule. PPMs don't usually cause vision problems, but if they are attached to the lens or cornea, they can cause opacity that will negatively affect a dog's vision. PPMs in young puppies are not a cause for concern, but if the puppy exam reveals a PPM, retesting at six-month intervals is recommended. If the PPM remains at one year of age, the dog should not be used for breeding.

Distachiasis is a condition in which one or more eyelashes grow inward toward the cornea. If not treated, the hair can cause corneal abrasions, which are very painful and potentially blinding. Distachiasis can be corrected surgically, but that is expensive. The mode of inheritance is unknown, but affected dogs should not be bred.

Hyaloid arteries, like PPMs, are tiny blood vessels that feed the embryonic eye. They are supposed to resolve, but sometimes part or all of the artery remains after birth. If they remain attached to the lens, a cataract may form at the point of attachment, and if so, the cataract will progress and cause blindness. Whether or not hyaloid arteries are hereditary has not been determined for certain.

Deafness

Congenital deafness, full or partial, occurs in Aussies, particularly those with white on or around their ears. What does white hair have to do with hearing? Pigment cells are important for translating sound waves into electrical impulses that can be transmitted by nerves to the brain. When pigment is lacking in the ear, the message—the sound—never reaches the brain. The dog cannot hear.

Deaf dogs can live happy lives, but they require very special owners. They can be trained to obey hand signals, but require extra vigilance, because they cannot hear danger approaching. They require patience because they cannot hear you calling, and they may startle more easily than hearing dogs—startled dogs sometimes bite. White Aussies are beautiful, but before acquiring one, have his hearing checked with a BAER test, and if he cannot hear, think very carefully about whether you can offer him not only love, but proper protection and care. Of course, Aussies suffering from deafness should never be bred.

Heart Disease

Patent ductus arteriosis (PDA) and the related but less serious condition, ductus diverticulum, are genetic heart defects. During fetal development, blood does not need to circulate through the lungs; the fetus gets its oxygen from the mother's blood. A shunt carries blood past the lungs. Once the puppy is born and begins to breathe, blood must pass through the lungs to extract oxygen. In PDA, the fetal shunt fails to resolve or go away, and part of the blood continues to bypass the lungs. The severity of PDA in an individual depends on how much blood is missing the lungs; it can range from mild to lethal. In ductus diverticulum, the shunt remains but is sealed and does not carry blood, so the blood gets properly oxygenated.

PDA causes a heart murmur, and murmurs are easily detected in puppies. Aussie pups should be checked for heart murmurs, preferably before they leave the breeder. Not every murmur indicates PDA, and some murmurs disappear with growth. If the pup still has a heart murmur at six months of age or has other symptoms of heart problems, he should be checked to determine the cause.

Epilepsy

Canine epilepsy is characterized by seizures or "fits," but not all seizures indicate epilepsy. Seizures are caused by a sudden, uncontrolled "firing" of nerves in the brain that causes repeated contraction of muscles. Seizures can be caused by exposure to toxic chemicals, drug sensitivities, injuries to the head, or disease. When no clear cause can be established for seizures, they are usually deemed to be symptoms of *idiopathic epilepsy*, which is considered to be genetic. Dogs with idiopathic epilepsy usually have their first seizures between one and five years of age.

Seizures are rarely fatal, but they are terrifying to watch, and a seizuring dog can injure himself when thrashing around. In extreme cases, a dog may experience continuous, uncontrollable seizures that can lead to secondary problems including hyperthermia, hypoglycemia, exhaustion, brain damage, and even death.

In most cases, seizures can be controlled with medication, but dogs that have epilepsy or have produced multiple offspring with epilepsy should not be bred.

Australian Shepherd owners should also note that some Aussies are sensitive to the drug Ivermectin, which is used to prevent or treat heartworm infection. Ivermectin will cause seizures in those individuals, so alternate heartworm prevention should be used.

Your Australian Shepherd will be a valued member of the family for a long time, so you'll want to ensure that he enjoys good health and a quality lifestyle.

Index